Rich as You Want to Be

Pay Attention Kids and Young People

Your future can be great.

By

Charles D. Calhoun

ISBN 978-1-7342197-0-8

Rich as You Want to Be

Pay Attention Kids and Young People

By

Charles D. Calhoun

DEDICATION

Did anyone ever tell you that you can be as rich as you chose to be? Probably not. In this book we will explain that and how to do that. So, read on.

Much of what every high school student needs to know about money is in this book. Middle school students can understand these ideas as well as they are not difficult to understand and use.

Like growing the tree on the cover, building wealth takes time. We all have time.

Why choose to be rich? Are you kidding? Everyone would choose to be rich if given the chance. We actually are given that choice, but we don't choose by answering that question. We decide by choosing the behaviors every day that lead toward wealth. They are simple and obvious steps and choices. So simple that they are easy to overlook, and most people do. Here are some of the right choices:

1. Do well or your best in school and get the best education that you can. Definitely finish high school. Post secondary (after high school: college or technical school) can double your income and more than double it depending on what you study.

2. Save for a rainy day. It will rain, guaranteed. Live within your means. This means you spend less than you earn. The difference you save and invest.

3. Avoid debt like the plague (a disease). Debt works against you, prevents becoming rich and can impoverish and even bankrupt you. Stay away. Realize there are very smart people working everyday to sell you debt so that they can have your money. Instead you should keep your money and avoid debt. It is your income or money that when invested will make you rich. That shiny new car will not promote wealth, and in fact will work against you becoming wealthy. So, save up and pay cash for what you want.

That is the least painful way to buy things.

4. Learn to become a good saver and investor. It really is not difficult just requiring you to be intentional with your money and to read a couple of books, and to talk to some successful people and keep your eyes and ears open.

5. Do what is right morally. Marry before having children. And stay married. Pick carefully. It is a very important choice not to be taken lightly.

And of course, there are behaviors to be avoided. We discuss some of these in our chapter about "pitfalls".

Why money? Money touches everything in our lives. Enough money enhances our liberty and makes us freer to use our time as we want. The lack of money on the other hand reduces our liberty and choices, forces us to live a less enjoyable lifestyle and makes us surrender our time to jobs and work. Don't get me wrong, working can be a very rewarding and even fun endeavor. And for most people when you need money for living expenses a job becomes a necessity.

You could read in the newspaper any week about young Americans carrying guns and shooting each other. They are often city dwellers and often poor. They may feel their opportunities are limited. Huge mistake. They live in the richest country the world has ever seen. There are opportunities virtually everywhere. And anyone can produce a good life and even become a millionaire. The shame is that typically folks don't know how to do that. Becoming financially successful is simple. It is a shame that our schools don't teach all students the simple steps to become financially successful and even wealthy. In this book I will spell out some ways anyone can do that. I have to think that if youngsters understood their opportunity there is no way they would throw it all away with violence or criminal activity.

Why are most people not rich, prosperous or even comfortable with enough money? There are a number of reasons. And understand, you can do very well with money. You can have enough, be rich, be financially independent and a millionaire.

This book will describe some ways you can help that happen as you build your future and your life.

Debt is one reason why more people don't prosper with money. I've read the average American pays $ 600,000 in interest payments over their lifetime. Interest paid is the cost of having debt. That is a TON of money and leaves far less to save and invest. Maybe that is why the median savings near retirement age (55 – 65) is only $ 3,000. And 25% of those people have $0. Debt and interest payments are to be avoided so YOU can win with money. Why not use that $ 600,000 to save, invest and build wealth? If instead you were to invest that $600,000 over 40 years what would that become? That would be $1,250 per month and at the end of 40 years your account would be worth $14.8 million dollars or thereabouts.

High school students and other young people have lots of advantages. Your future is in front of you. And your future has lots of years with which you can be productive. Those years are very valuable as time is one of the ingredients necessary to build wealth in most cases.

You may also have much of your education in front of you and can chose to make the most of that too. Be the best student you can be and chose fields of study that you love and that offer the chance to produce good income.

Recent studies reveal that most young people don't receive good financial education and that they wish they had while in school. That is a shame because the ideas are teachable, are really pretty simple and are very useful as well as profitable. These are ideas that can be used every day to improve your life, your future and the well being of your family and other loved ones.

Why not be rich? Really why not?

You can become financially well off. You can build enough wealth to have financial independence and never need to work for money again, and even become a millionaire. You can do it and it's simple to do. It's simple yet most people do not do it. Why is that? We believe there are several key reasons why it is rarer than one would think. You would expect everyone to want to be prosperous. Why aren't most people? First, many people are never shown how to do that. This book will show how. Secondly, just because it is simple doesn't mean it's easy. And for many people it is difficult to do. Why is that? It takes work and doing the right things over a long period of time in most cases. Doing the right things will mean living within your means or spending less than is earned. And thirdly, it is very easy to get into debt and lose control of your income. Car loans, college loans and credit cards are all easy to obtain and the temptation to buy nice things is ever present. But debt is not so easy to pay off. It's easy to spend too much on shiny stuff or on a million other things but painful to pay it off. So people tend to accumulate debt instead of assets. And then they must pay interest and lose some of their income.

Anyone can improve their financial position. You can do that in a heartbeat. Just decide to not spend what you do not have or cut up those credit cards for example. Many people spend decades building wealth by working, saving and investing. Most others never get around to saving or investing. Time will pass regardless what you do, and one day those years will be behind you. I would guess that when you reach an older age you would like to be both healthy and wealthy. This book may help you do both. These ideas are not secret yet are often not learned in most schools. The result is that some of these ideas remain unknown to most people. Therefore, they can't use them. There is a true statement that, "You don't know what you don't know." After you read this book you will know some of the things to do and your future could be brighter. Knowing is one thing. Action is required to make these ideas work. The actions are simple and often easy. Keep in mind that personal finance is 20% what you know but 80% behavior. What you do or don't do counts. A lot.

I'm sure the ideas in this book can greatly benefit young people. They can benefit the most from these ideas because they have the most years to let their investments grow. This book was written for them. They have the time to achieve the great things described in this book. Some of the best results described may happen

20, 30 or 40 years into the future. That may seem like an amount of time that will never pass. But it surely will. When your time is used as we suggest your future will be better, more enjoyable and who knows, maybe even rich.

Don't be discouraged if you are older. Even if you are a senior citizen your future is still in front of you and you can make progress. Colonel Sanders didn't even start KFC until he was collecting Social Security. Grandma Moses didn't paint her first painting until she was 85. Cool. So, let's all just begin where we are.

I'd further like to dedicate this book to my friend Rachael. Rachael and I trained as we ran long distances in the Rockefeller Preserve as she prepared for her college cross-country seasons. It was then that I realized that it is young people who could benefit most from these ideas and that is what inspired me to write this book to provide key information to them.

Charlie Calhoun

CONTENTS

INTRODUCTION: RICH AS YOU WANT TO BE

Money isn't everything, but lack of money sure is no fun. Being broke is so common it is "normal". Don't be normal. Instead be unusual or weird, and wealthy. And it is all doable. And I mean by you.

What exactly is a "MILLIONAIRE"?

A millionaire is a person with net worth of more than $1 million. That used to mean you were rich. Dollars today are worth less than they were in the past. So, a million dollars' worth of assets is not worth today what it was decades ago. Of course, you would also have to subtract what is owed (debts) from their assets to calculate their NET WORTH. Here are a couple of examples for fun:

A. Assets $450,000 investments and cash plus $750,000 house and no debts = $1.2 million net worth and a millionaire. While the house is an asset and REAL ESTATE, that part of it is hard to spend, but it can also go up (or down) in value.

B. Assets $450,000 investments and a

$750,000 house, but they owe $400,000 on the house. $1.2 million in assets minus $400,000 owed equals a net worth of "only" $800,000. Not a millionaire but soon could be one.

C. Assets of $20,000 but debts of $95,000 (car loan plus college loans plus credit cards). $20,000 minus $95,000 equals -$75,000 net worth. They would have to save and pay off debt of $75,000 just to get back to ZERO. Ouch! At that point they would be broke.

Me become a millionaire? Can I really do that?

Well, of course you can. If you invest a mere $100 each month once working from say age 20 to age 60 that would grow to be $1,188,242 and you would be a millionaire based on that alone. That should enable you to enjoy a fine life. It also gives you lots of choices, which is freedom. That first million could be invested and could turn into $2 million, $5 million, $10 million, or even $100 million. Who knows where it could lead? Each million could be used to produce income of roughly $50,000 per year or even more. Imagine if you had $5 million. That could produce an income of about $250,000 per year or about $20,000 per month. For most people, that would be a nice allowance. And the good news is that the steps required to do that are each really simple even easy. It just takes some time. But you have time. We all do.

I was very fortunate. Money wasn't the most important thing to me. But I did pay attention when money was the subject. I was very busy working in my career (as a teacher) and raising our family. Over time I have learned a few things about money and investing and have become a fairly successful investor. You could say I became wealthy, financially independent and a millionaire even though that wasn't an urgent goal for me.

Of course, you can do it!

Sadly, most people never learn lots of these ideas or figure it out. If only 3% become millionaires that means 97% don't. That is so unfortunate because it is so doable. The vast majority of people lose their most powerful wealth building tool, their income, by going into debt to buy things they want now instead of saving for it, waiting and paying cash. Being a net worth millionaire doesn't make you very rich, but you and your loved ones will be OK and probably comfortable.

Many are fooled by the mistaken idea that the government or someone else will provide for them. Nobody could provide for you as well as you could for yourself because they don't care about your welfare. Nobody cares about you or your loved ones as much as you do. Nor should they. They don't have the motivation. They don't know what your goals are. And they are too busy providing for themselves to care about your desires. Many others lose years and even decades before they hear of or learn these principles. The loss of that time prevents them from being as successful as they might have been had they known this essential information at a younger age.

The ideas explained in this book should be taught in schools but are not in most schools. They could be part of mathematics and can easily be understood by middle school aged children. Learning these ideas at an early age would offer advantages and would contribute to financial literacy. They could also go a long way toward preventing serious mistakes, bad choices or poverty. If your future is bright why would anyone want to ruin it with bad choices?

The ideas presented in this book are *simple* and fairly easy to understand. Equally important, they are doable by just about everybody. It isn't rocket science. Anyone can do this. It may not be overly easy to do in every case, but it sure is simple. I'm writing this book to share some of what I've learned in the hope that more people will better understand how to become financially successful so that they can provide a better life for themselves, their loved ones, and the people they care about.

Some millionaires make their millions by owning a business. Some become fabulously wealthy and seem to do it in a short amount of time. It usually takes lots of years to become such an "overnight" success. But when a person builds a fortune in a short time period, like five or ten years, it is usually through starting and running a business.

This book is written for the other people. The people who spend decades gradually building their fortune as they go about their business, raise their families, and live their normal lives. That would be most people. I'd say for the "normal" people except normal is broke even in America. Becoming financially independent is rare enough that Dave Ramsey refers to these people as "weird". But it is weird in a good way and a very good place to be.

It is especially written for students and young people. Young people are blessed with *lots of time*, boundless energy, and optimism that life has the promise of being great. And it does. Having lots of time is one of the key ingredients to building wealth. It's like growing a tree. It takes lots of time to do that. Building a fortune usually takes plenty of time too.

It is my hope that this book will inform, inspire, and perhaps help some to believe that you can do great things in your life. And better yet, this book will show how to do that.

These ideas are simple enough for middle

school and high school students to understand. I know that because I have shared them with students of that age. And they got it. And they were glad to learn these ideas. The practical benefits are obvious. I believe these concepts should be taught to all young people in school. To not do so is to promote financial illiteracy. And there is plenty of that. And that leads to problems of debt, poverty, despair, and loss of opportunity for many people. In the richest country on earth why should 97% of 65-year old's be unable to write a check for $600? That is the price people pay because they weren't taught the ideas in this little book. Or they didn't pursue them and learn them on their own.

It is also my wish to help young people avoid the mistakes that sometimes damage lives. There really can be a future that is wonderful and one you don't want to miss out on by falling into one of the pitfalls that damage lives. If you understood that in your future you would be wealthy and happy, would you gamble your life on cigarettes, drugs, or other dangerous activities? It would be wise not to.

The bottom line is that *you can do it*. It's simple. Simple but not always easy. You will be able to understand these ideas. They are easy to understand and, for most people, easily doable. It is not difficult to put your wealth building on autopilot. I hope these ideas help you to build a great future and that you become as successful as you desire. The sky is the limit.

CHAPTER 1: KEEP A POSITIVE ATTITUDE

Your attitude is your own creation. If it isn't great, make it so. Stay fired up! Expect only the best. Then work to make that happen.

If your attitude is bad it is on you. Fix it ASAP.

The good man reaps the fruit of his paths. Proverbs 14:14

Point number one is to keep a positive attitude. It's a fairly amazing reality that we choose our own attitude. We can choose to be optimistic, or we can choose to be discouraged and depressed. We have all met people who have chosen to be miserable. I can't explain that, but it's not for me. And I don't think it's for you either.

Here are a couple of useful ideas about attitude. Dale Carnegie makes a great point in his book called <u>How to Stop Worrying and Enjoy Your Life</u> when he says we are better off if we "count your blessings and not your troubles." That we are far better off if we pay more attention to those things that are right or great than to those that are imperfect or could be troubling.

An amazing reality is that there never was a person exactly like you in the whole history of the universe. There will never be another one. Each one of us is extremely fortunate to be here. Most of us are blessed in a number of ways.

One of the stories that I find very striking about attitude is the story of Victor Frankl. Victor Frankl was an inmate in a concentration camp. He tells his story in *Man's Search for Meaning*. He came to the realization that he had the absolute freedom to choose his own attitude. The Nazi guards couldn't choose it for him. He found that very liberating. Although he was locked in a concentration camp, he felt free because he could choose his own attitude. I don't know that I'd be able to choose such a positive attitude under those circumstances. (His young wife was gassed and murdered upon arrival at concentration camp). It does show you what the potential is and what some of the possibilities are. In reality if you live in the United States you are already rich. If the nation you live in is at peace you are indeed blessed. If you are a free person and not a slave count your blessings and be grateful because millions have been slaves. If you are protected by armed police and military thank them every chance you get because you are safe from many harms.

Dale Carnegie, in another of his books (*How to Win Friends and Influence People*), discusses what people look for in other people or what people like in other people. He lists four or five things that people like. We can all do these things. He says to smile. It makes sense that people would be more likely to like a person with a smiling face. Or as I would tell my students, "My number one beauty tip is to smile."

Another item was to listen well. People like other people who listen well. If you smile and listen well, there is a good chance that people will like you and treat you well. That can help you enjoy your life and maintain your positive attitude. It is easy to have a positive attitude when people like you and are kind to you. Just doing those two things which we can all do will lead to more friends, better grades and higher paying jobs.

I also believe that if you show great manners and consideration to people, they will appreciate that and will treat you well. This is true in most cases, but not all.

But even if people are unkind to you or circumstances are difficult, you still have the ability to choose your own attitude. And if you are mobile, you can stay away from people who are unpleasant or negative, which is not a bad thing to do.

Art Williams, in his book *All You Can Do Is All You Can Do*, talks about how to be successful. He lists three things you can do. They are the following:

1. **Do what is right**. If you do what is right, the results tend to be very good. And if you do what is wrong, sometimes very bad things happen. Recently, young Paris Hilton was sent to jail. She made the mistake of drinking alcohol and driving her car. She later drove her car under the influence when her license was suspended. That's asking for trouble. And she looked pretty unhappy when she was sent to jail. Jails are full

of people who failed to do what is right. Do what is right, and enjoy the positive results.

His second point was to:

2. **Work hard**. If you work hard, success is virtually assured. If you work hard, you will outwork 50 percent, if not 90 percent, of other people. It's not a competition against other people. It's just that if you work hard, you will find yourself in the upper echelons of achievement in whatever area you are working in because the reality is that most people do not work hard all the time.

Lamp made by the author.

The above lamp is beautiful. You can imagine the amount of work in cutting individually each of the

1,986 pieces of glass and then assembling the lamp. It was hard work but an outstanding result that can now be enjoyed every day for years or even decades.

The third step that he recommends is to:

3. **Treat people great.** So many of the best things that happen in life are the result of treating people great. When you treat people great, they often return the favor. And we all enjoy being treated well. There is great personal satisfaction that comes with doing what is right and best. One good deed deserves another.

Let me summarize that three-point recipe for success:

1. Always *do what is right.*

2. *Work hard* and do your best.

3. *Treat people great.*

If you do those three things, you will be very successful. Simply doing these things and living in this manner makes you a success regardless of other outcomes in your life and career. When you become financially successful that can make it easier to keep a positive attitude. And a positive attitude just attracts good things to you and makes your life more enjoyable in the first place. Doing these things may also remove stress from your life.

But also remember that even if bad fortune comes your way, it doesn't control your attitude. You can still maintain an attitude that is a positive attitude even under difficult circumstances.

See the glass as half full not half empty. Optimism is the better, happier way to live.

Main point:

Your attitude is your creation. It is your task to make it great and keep it great. It's easy to do. It's fun. And it rewards you. A positive attitude attracts good people and things to you.

CHAPTER 2: GET THE BEST EDUCATION THAT YOU CAN

You don't know what you don't know. But learning, education and knowledge can surely help you make a better future. "Momma said, Stupid is as stupid does." Not completing your education or not doing your best would be unwise. It is not wise to sell your education short! You got this! And you can do this well. Give it your very best effort.

Wise men store up knowledge. Proverbs 10:14

Step number two is to get the best education that you can. I know, for young people, sometimes it seems very difficult to go to school. It can be challenging. Sometimes the courses required are not the most exciting things in the world. And there are other things to do that might seem more enjoyable. But education pays and pays well.

Educational level is directly related to income. Education opens doors to higher income. In the US census, this is shown very clearly. Median incomes in 2006 show the following approximations:

High school dropouts earn $553 per week or $28,756 per year on average.

High school graduates earn $730 per week or $37,960 per year on average.

College graduates earn $1,200 per week or $62,400 per year on average.

People with Graduate degrees can earn $1,500 and up per week or $75,000 plus per year on average. Median household income in the US in 2017 was $61,372. Average salary in USA is just $47,060 in 2019 and is generally higher for older Americans. Be above average. Even with that average income you can still become wealthy, financially independent and a millionaire.

And remember an average number gives you information but there are no guarantees. For example, if the average number of children is 2.3 per family that informs you. But there is no family with 2.3 children.

The odd thing is that the college grads don't need to work as hard physically as the high school dropouts. High school dropouts very often have to work two jobs just to meet their expenses, in order to just survive. They may also have to take jobs that are physically strenuous, dirty, unpleasant or hazardous. While school may seem difficult, education does often lead to an easier, more pleasant, richer and more rewarding life.

The better your education the more jobs you get to choose from. It would make sense that with a better education you will choose a better higher paying and more enjoyable job.

In addition, those with the lower level of education often have to settle for the most difficult, dirty and sometimes dangerous work in order to earn a living. They might find themselves doing landscaping or roofing. These are jobs out in the sun that are very strenuous and can be unpleasant. Once in such a job a person may realize that school might be an easier and much more promising route.

High school graduates may choose from less strenuous more pleasant and rewarding jobs. The high school graduate may work for a utility company or drive a truck making FedEx deliveries where he may be earning $800 to $1,000 per week or more. Which enables a person to meet their expenses with a single job and probably have a good retirement plan growing. The low-income individual has a much more difficult time saving. And saving is what really creates financial independence down the line. Without saving and investing it is difficult to build wealth or a fortune.

College graduates often earn between $1,000 and $2,000 per week. And they would be working in professions where there is much less manual labor. There is much less sweat, or danger involved. They could be teachers or accountants for example. These are jobs that a lot of people enjoy. They pay well and are respected professions. Teaching is not as easy as people think, until they have actually done it themselves. It's a very rewarding profession. A good teacher will enhance the lives of thousands of children.

Graduate school graduates are people who have continued their education even after completing four years of college. They tend to go into professions. They could be doctors, lawyers, CEO's of companies, managers, and they can earn incomes of $100,000 and up. There are graduates coming out of business schools who earn $150,000 and $200,000 to start. There is no upper limit on income in free market economies such as ours. There are people who earn tens and even hundreds of millions of dollars in a single year. One of the Walton heirs (Walmart) earned $220,000,000 in dividends in a recent six month period. That was just a part of her income.

When you think of the high school dropout or even the high school graduate working to earn $25,000 or $35,000 per year and you compare that with earning $200,000 per year, well, it's a fairly huge difference. The question you might want to ask yourself is, "Would you rather work and earn $200,000 a year, which breaks out to be about $4,000 per week? Or would you rather earn $30,000 per year ($600 per week), which could be gone as soon as you pay your basic bills, leaving you little money to save and invest?" You would probably need a second job just to have the money needed to enjoy your life or to save for a better future.

The question you may want to ask yourself might be, "Which income would I choose for myself if given the choice?"

Would I choose $600 per week? Or would I choose $4,000 per week? Not a difficult choice.

Of course, everyone will pick the larger amount. But the choice isn't spelled out in such direct terms. But it is influenced and even determined by how far you choose to go in your education, and what talents and learned skills you bring to the job.

What I would advise young people is to get the best education you can. Discipline yourself to do well in school. You will not be sorry that you did. The better you do in school and the further you go in your education, the richer your life will most probably be and the more satisfying your life will be because the higher you go on the educational ladder, the more options are open to you. The lower your educational level, the fewer choices you may have. And often those choices are not as pleasant. They may be jobs that are open because nobody wants them.

Another problem with small incomes is that saving, and investing is much more difficult with a small income. Saving and investing is an essential key to building wealth. It is very desirable to produce a higher income. But even if a person has a relatively small income, there is still hope. Should such a person live a careful and disciplined lifestyle and make saving a priority, they too can produce a financially secure future. We all must live on less than we earn to build wealth. In fact, it is still possible to build financial independence and even become a millionaire, as we will describe in this book. We will spell out exactly how to do just that.

There are many examples of very successful people who made their fortunes while working after not finishing their educations. Some of the richest people in America are in fact on this list.

<u>Main point:</u>

Get the best education you can and that will probably enable you to obtain the best income you can. It's never too late to add to your education.

CHAPTER 3: AVOID THE PITFALLS

Or

BETTER SAFE THAN SORRY

Keep your eyes open and watch your step. Thirteen thousand Americans are killed each year simply by slipping and falling down. Watch out for those banana peels and ice patches. Bad things happen when people don't pay attention. Stay alert. Eyeballs, click!

He who is impulsive exalts folly. Proverbs 14:29

Never rush. Haste makes waste.

While most of this book is going to recommend things, you can do to help you enjoy a happy and successful financial life, we should spend a few moments to discuss avoiding pitfalls. Because you can do most everything that's right in terms of providing for your success, but there are some mistakes that people make that can interfere with or delay their success. This chapter will suggest that point number three is to avoid the pitfalls. Avoid the dangers that can appear at any moment. Keep your eyes open. Stay alert and try to avoid them. Here are a couple of them.

Drug use is a big problem. Drugs are substances that can harm a person. Illegal drugs are especially dangerous. They can enslave a person with addiction or worse yet, cause a sudden death by "overdose". There has been a huge increase in heroin overdose deaths all across our country. It is as if someone is trying to poison our young people. And of course, drug cartels could care less who they harm. Each of us has to be informed enough and principled enough to never use drugs.

There are more than enough ways to feel good, and ways that produce positive outcomes as well as good feelings. I would include exercise (strength and fitness), sports (fun, friendships, excitement, memories), working hard in many areas (school success, hobbies, music, art and the list is almost endless). There are lots of ways to feel good while also doing what is both right and productive.

Even prescription drugs under a doctor's supervision can have harmful side effects. Likewise, over the counter drugs. In general, we are better off without them.

Smoking cigarettes has the potential of shortening a person's life by a great deal. In fact, not only shorten a person's life but also make them sick in many ways. I know we do see some young people who smoke, and they imagine, "If I get cancer in twenty years when I'm forty, I'll be an old fogy at that point in time." Or more commonly, "Cancer happens, but it won't happen to me." It is amazing how time passes, and before you know it, you are forty years old, and you have a couple of young children running around your beautiful home. I promise you that you won't want to be sick at that time or any time. You will want to be as healthy as can be, so you can enjoy your life and your family for 100 years or more.

Another pitfall is drinking alcohol to excess. This is especially dangerous when in combination with driving a motor vehicle. Forget about it! When I think of my friends who died at an early age, usually drinking and driving was involved. I grew up during the Vietnam War era, but all of my friends who died at an early age died as a result of drinking alcohol and driving a car, not warfare. In most cases, they also were not wearing a seat belt. Of course, they did have an excuse as most cars had no seat belts in the 1960s. But today, always wear your seat belt. Accidents do not announce themselves in advance. You never know when an accident may suddenly happen. They appear out of the blue in an instant. Stay away from the alcohol, particularly when driving. And always wear that seat belt. When people are killed in car accidents, they often are not wearing a seatbelt. Princess Diana was rich and famous and beautiful. But she rode in a speeding car driven by a driver who had consumed alcohol. She was killed in the crash. Sometimes it takes a single mistake to end your dreams and even your life. And the mistakes were the driver's not even hers.

Many of the people who make mistakes and go to jail or prison made their mistakes while under the influence of alcohol or drugs. It might be as high as 75% of those who commit crimes and get convicted. Alcohol and drugs both lead to poor decisions.

You can further reduce the number of car accidents and their severity by obeying traffic rules, especially the speeding laws. I know that speed can be exciting sometimes, but when you drive just a bit slower, you have more time to react in order to avoid an accident. And an accident at a slower rate of speed also does much less damage to cars and to the people in the cars. Never rush when driving and understand that there is truth in such sayings as, "Speed kills" and "Haste makes waste."

Young people, or should I say, new drivers should also be humble and understand that it takes time and practice to become an excellent driver and a very safe driver. For most drivers that takes months and even years of practice. It is also true that in the beginning you will be a more dangerous driver. Remember that in most things, "Before you can be great, you have to be good. And before you are good [at driving], you will be bad or a beginner or less skilled." That is the normal progression in learning most things.

Young people are sometimes unaware of the dangers associated with driving because it looks so easy to do. New drivers may also suffer from premature overconfidence.

There are other things that are dangerous. If you look around, you will see there are some people who are dangerous. There are people who are violent, negative, or destructive. There are people who have bad habits or values. It would be wise to stay away from those people as far as possible.

There are dangerous activities. Pay attention and you will see examples of errors and accidents that happen. They are in the newspapers and on the TV news virtually every day. It is important to be observant, careful and thoughtful and take care to avoid injuries. My son at one point had a motorcycle, and he used to like to drive it fast. He was a speed merchant who liked to go very fast. It scared me to death. And I didn't even know he went 140 miles per hour and even faster until later on. He came within a hair's breadth of being killed. He was in an accident where his shoulder was split in half. Fortunately for him, there was an EMT guy right on the scene who was able to give him first aid. He was also lucky that when his accident happened, he wasn't going very fast. The accident happened only five minutes from the medical center. He survived. He was fortunate to survive. He is fine today, I'm happy to report. Other motorcycle riders are not always so lucky. Today he has a lovely family and all his limbs.

You may want to ask yourself if riding a motorcycle and the thrill of speed is worth losing your life over. And there are many things that people engage in that have the ability to end their dreams with one mistake and in an instant. So those things are to be avoided.

A shocking fact that I teach my students is that 13,000 Americans die as a result of tripping and falling down each year in America. I tell them to "watch their step" or you might trip or "slip on a banana peel". They don't know what that means because they have probably never seen a banana peel on the ground, but when I was a child, they were very common. Back then people littered more than today and didn't pick up after their dogs either and it was common to "step in it" and get to clean off your shoe. Gross. I guess you could slip on that too. Keep those eyes open and "watch your step." Recently a friend of mine was injured when he fell down after slipping on a wet spot his dog made on the floor.

There are also a number of financial pitfalls such as accidents, disability and death. These will be discussed in Chapter 10.

Point number three is to stay alert and keep your eyes open to avoid the dangers or pitfalls that exist. Those dangers can destroy your dreams, your health, your life, and possibly ruin the lives of your children as well. Had my son died in that motorcycle accident, his two children who were born after that event would not have been born.

Try to learn from your mistakes and even the mistakes other people make.

Main point: Better safe than sorry.

CHAPTER 4: AVOID DEBT

Debt hurts you. Avoid it because it harms you and your future. Most people have debt. It is being marketed to us every day, but it hurts people, almost every time.

The rich rule over the poor, and the borrower is slave to the lender. Proverbs 22:7

And. Owe no one anything, except to love one another. Romans 13:8

Be an adult and pay for your stuff!

What is debt and how does it happen? And how can you prevent yourself from having debt?

Debt is like bleeding except what is being lost is your money or income rather than blood. But the first rule of First Aid is to STOP THE BLEEDING. You can prevent that "bleeding" by avoiding debt and by getting rid of it as soon as possible if you have any.

It is easy to take on debt. All one needs to do is sign that paper and get that shiny new car with those "low monthly payments". Most people do just that. There are lots and lots of temptations to encourage you to spend more than you earn. To get that item now instead of waiting "years" while you save for it. There are credit cards all over the place, shiny beautiful cars that can be yours just for signing the application. It seems almost too easy. The payments (the hard part) come later and can last for years. College loan payments can last for decades. Ouch!

Those are very important questions. In the Dedication I wondered why more people do not become wealthy since it seems to be simple to do. One of the main reasons is because most people have debt. Debt is "normal". They owe money for things they have bought when they couldn't pay cash for it. It could be a car, a college education, a pair of pants, or a repair of an appliance. As a result, they must spend their income paying back debt plus INTEREST to the person or institution they owe money to. Often this leaves them without the money to save, invest and build wealth.

Some of the common ways people get into debt include the following:

1. **Credit cards** are plastic cards used to charge expenses when purchases are made. When you use a credit card it is easy and painless to spend money so people sometimes spend more than they should. Ideally it is best to actually feel it when you spend money. That helps prevent overspending and going into debt. When you have credit card debt you have to pay back the money borrowed plus INTEREST. INTEREST is money charged for using their money to make your purchase. Interest rates can vary and can be 8%, 12%, 18%, 22% or 28% per year. These charges can add up especially if you have a large balance to pay. It is easy to see a credit card balance grow. It is easy to want stuff and it can be fun to buy but not so much fun to pay it back. Therefore, many people don't rush to pay it back. And therefore, the debt will grow by adding new purchases and due to the interest that builds up. American consumers owe more than 1.1 trillion dollars for credit card purchases. That is $ 1,100,000,000,000.00. Wow! That

is a lot of zeros. If 100 million people owe that total it means the average debt is about $ 11,000 each. And that means that if the interest rate is 20%, the balance will grow by $2,200 per year for each person even when no new purchases occur. And new purchases do happen, sometimes daily.

People are encouraged to use credit cards by banks, retail stores, TV commercials and in other ways. These companies make lots of money when people use these cards and take on debt. This is a perfect example of how it is easy even seemingly fun to go into debt. But it takes hard work to get out of debt.

2. **Car loans** are used to help people buy new cars. New cars are very nice and fun too. But they are expensive. It is common for a purchaser to borrow money to pay for the car and then pay it off over 3,4,5, or 6 years. New Cars are fun but car loan payments are no fun. They also use up your money which might prevent you from saving and

investing and building wealth for your future. There is about $1.1 trillion in car loan debt. If 40 million people owe that the average debt is about $ 27,500 each. The total owed has increased 38% over the past five years as cars have become more expensive to buy. In today's newspaper it was pointed out that the average car payment is $503 per month for 68 months. That cannot be fun.

3. **College loans** are used to help pay for college. And we all know that a college education helps increase your earnings in the future. But that is true if you borrow money to pay for it or if you never borrow a penny before you graduate. Having it paid for is the best way to go. Borrowing leads to debt, interest payments and other problems. Student loan debt stands at about $ 1.6 trillion (That is $1,600,000,000,000) and is up 37% over the past five years. Like cars, colleges just keep raising their prices and usually faster than the rate of inflation. If that $1.6 trillion is owed by

20 million graduates, that would be $80,000 each. It would take payments of $669 per month for 20 YEARS to pay off that loan if the interest rate was 8% per year. Are you kidding me?

And of course, there are other ways to borrow and get into debt. It is easy and quite "normal" to get into debt. And while it may be common, it is extremely unwise and to be avoided if at all possible. And it is possible. It's hard to pay off any debt and get out of debt. The above three examples are just the most common types.

What would life look like for an average person who is "normal" and has all three of these debts? Their payments might look like this:

1. Credit card with $ 10,000 debt would require a payment of $329 per month for 3 years @ 12% interest to pay it off, that is if they didn't add more purchases to the account. It is easy and common to add more purchases.
2. Car loan of $ 27,500 could be paid off at 8% interest for $667 per month for 4 years, or

$479 per month for six years. **Ouch! T**hat would surely hurt!

3. A Student loan of $70,000 could be paid off in 20 years at 5% interest for a mere $ 460 per month. Are you kidding me? Twenty years?? But if the interest rate was 8%, the payments would be $585.51 per month for twenty years. Nobody wants to do that!!

   Seems crazy but many (most?) people do these unwise things. As the Bible says, "The borrower is slave to the lender."

If a person was "unlucky" enough to have all three of the above they would pay each month:

Debt Type	Monthly Payment	Time
Credit card(s)	$ 329 for 3 years	
Car loan	$ 667 for 4 years	
Student loan	$ 460 for 20 years	

Total each month $ 1,456

Oh boy! How would you like to make these payments every month FOR YEARS? OUCH! Debts like those above might help explain why so many people don't save and invest enough to become prosperous. Their income goes to pay debts and therefore it is not available to invest.

Put another way would you not prefer to put $1,456 into your savings account each month? That amount each month saved and invested for 30 years at 12% return would total **5 MILLION DOLLARS**. And what would be the point of having FIVE MILLION DOLLARS invested? You would surely be financially independent and only working for the enjoyment of it. If you chose to take 7% as an income from that $5 million, that would pay you $ 350,000 per year or roughly $30,000 per month. Wouldn't that be a lot better than owing debt? You Bet!

But if you are careful and wise you can avoid all the above debts and the <u>painful payments</u> to get rid of those debts. It is easy to take on debts but HARD and not fun to pay back that money. The keys are to spend only what you have. Don't borrow money. Live on less than you earn. And save money. Save money for expenses you know are coming. Money saved is the best way to pay for big expenses. When you borrow, the payments you must make follow you home. If you don't borrow, there are no future payments or interest expenses at all. And then your money can be used for your purposes, goals and things you will enjoy.

Make it a priority to avoid DEBT whenever possible.

Money issues are the number one cause of stress and also divorce. DEBT causes lack of money and bill paying stress. Abundant cash does not cause stress, at least for me.

So how does one get rid of debt?

If like most people, you are "normal" and already have some debts; how do you then get rid of them? I like the approach taught by Dave Ramsey, and he should know having guided millions of people to become **"debt free"**. Typically, that means all debts paid off except home mortgage. You can hear all about his **"baby steps" for paying off debt and becoming debt free. And by the way,** you can learn these steps by listening to Dave Ramsey's free podcasts or You Tube videos, or by reading his books such as **(THE TOTAL MONEY MAKEOVER)** or by taking his course (Financial Peace University).

Some of Dave's baby steps are below as I understand them. Do them in this order.

1. Set up an emergency fund with just $1,000 in it. All other savings (other than retirement investments) are then directed at debts.

2. After that, Direct all possible moneys at

your debts. Develop "gazelle intensity" because it is hard to pay off debts and your financial life and financial peace is at stake. Gazelles in the wild become intense to escape cheetahs who hunt them because their life depends on it. Seek ways to produce extra income as debt is paid off. It can be overtime, a part time job or selling things you own (like that expensive car).

3. After that, Build an emergency fund of 3 to 6 months expenses. Keep these funds liquid in money market funds so they are available in case of an emergency.

4. After that, Fund your retirement savings fund with 15% of your household income. That can be 401k, IRA, Roth IRA, 403b, 457 or other retirement account. These are all great ways to grow your wealth.

5. To learn more about Dave Ramsey's Baby steps and approach see his YouTube videos, listen to his pod casts or read his books.

Paying off debt is hard work and typically requires behavior changes, writing a monthly budget (with both spouses when married), determination, being intentional (is a weird idea right? Actually, doing what you intend to do) and may even require some PLASTIC SURGERY (as in cutting up those plastic credit cards). But the payoff is huge. Living debt free actually means having money and sometimes lots more money. It is then easy to live on less than you earn. You will then also be able to save, invest and build greater wealth. You may even become financially independent and a millionaire. Who knew that getting rid of debt was a key to financial and even life style success? Most people never realize that as we have credit (actually debt) marketed to us constantly. You sacrifice to pay off those debts living on **"rice and beans"** and **"never seeing the inside of a restaurant unless you WORK THERE!"** Or as Dave Ramsey famously says, **you "live like no one else so that later you can live and give like no one else!"**

Main point: Dave Ramsey is right. Don't become enslaved to debt.

CHAPTER 5: PREPARE FOR "EMERGENCIES"

Get ready. Emergencies happen all the time.

Motto of the Boy Scouts of America is, *"Be prepared".*
Preparation is on you. That is YOUR job!

The easiest way to fix many problems is to write a check, providing that you have the funds ready and waiting.

There is a saying known as Murphy's law. It states, "Whatever can go wrong, will go wrong." And often when that happens it happens at the worst time. As you will find out, these unexpected emergencies happen pretty often. So often in fact, that we all need to be prepared for them. They will happen whether we are ready or not.

Some examples would be the car needs repair, there is a car accident, any accident causing injury, a sickness, the roof leaks, child needs braces, a major appliance needs replacement (dish washer, water heater, washing machine, refrigerator etc.). Life happens. And with these emergencies comes expense. If you don't have savings handy it puts you in the position of having to borrow the money needed to correct the problem. Then the person would have two problems instead of one.

One way to prepare for emergencies is to build an "emergency fund" of three to six months of expenses.

Let's say that your normal expenses are $5,000 per month. Three months of expenses would be $15,000 and six months would be 6 x $5,000 or $30,000.

Let's say you have $15,000 in your emergency fund and your car needs an $800 repair. Easy, just write a check. Or maybe your water heater fails and needs replacing for $1,000. No problem just write a check. Or maybe they both happen in the same week. No problem just write two checks. Without the emergency fund you might have to choose from options that hurt you. You could use a charge card and take on some debt. Or you could withdraw from an IRA or other retirement account and have to pay taxes plus penalties. Clearly having the money already sitting in your emergency fund would be the most comfortable and least expensive way to handle these or any emergency.

The reality is that unexpected expenses pop up all the time. Be prepared with an emergency fund and you will handle your emergencies with ease, and not create another problem such as debt and interest payments. Save for that rainy day. It will rain. Guaranteed!!

Main point: Life happens. Prepare for it.

CHAPTER 6: SAVE MONEY

FROM ZERO TO A HERO

In the house of the wise are stores of choice food and oil, but a foolish man devours all he has. Proverbs 21:20

Live on less than you earn, and you will never be broke, and may wake up wealthy someday. That means save for your future needs. Strive to save money. Make saving a priority and something you do on purpose whenever you get paid. We all begin life broke, but don't need to stay that way.

We all begin life broke. Babies are born in a state of poverty and then pass through a childhood of 12 to 18 years without any income to speak of. Fortunate children have a home with loving parents and a secure environment to grow and mature in. But almost all of us begin at $0 and need to work and make income to begin our savings journey. Some people never save and remain broke for life. Some others develop large incomes and build fortunes. But what can the average or ordinary person do? Fortunately, it doesn't take a fortune to build a fortune. Small regular, affordable contributions invested in equity mutual funds over decades of time can grow into millions. And that is enough to be rich and have a rich life. It is very doable, and we are about to show you how. If you are young that is a great advantage and means you have lots of time. Time is one of the key ingredients needed to grow your investments and wealth. If you are older you may still have lots of time. You probably have 30 or more years and can still do big things.

If you don't put money away for your future, who do you expect will do that for you? Remember that things will happen. There will be future expenses, even some unexpected ones. Christmas will come this December, again.

Everyone would like to be a millionaire. But when they think of saving ten million dollars or even one million dollars, most think, "That isn't possible." Or, "I could never do that. So why try?" In this chapter, we will show you how to do exactly that. Pretty much anyone who works can save $100 per month. $100 per month for 40 years (lets say ages 22 to 62) invested in mutual funds averaging 12% annual return would grow to be worth about $1.2 MILLION! And it is simple. You really don't need to save millions. You could begin with a small account. That in turn could grow into a much larger account, even a million-dollar account. Perhaps saving is not always easy, but simple it is. Just open a savings account and set up automatic deposits from your checking account or by payroll deduction from your job. Payroll deduction is among the **very best ways to save.** Once your signup the saving is automatic, and you never handle that money. You may have noticed that cash you receive in your hands will usually vanish as it gets spent. Money you never touch removes that temptation, and thus the money goes where you intend it to go, on purpose.

Not everyone will succeed. But everyone can succeed. If you don't try, you certainly won't save much. Money is just too easy to spend. When you do try you may fall short but will still be better off and maybe financially independent. Would you feel bad if you had "only" $800,000 worth of assets? You could be wealthy at that level depending on your needs. Sure, would beat $0.

But suppose you fall short and "only" build

investments or savings worth $ 500,000 or $ 700,000. Depending on your needs you may then be financially independent or prosperous anyway. It would depend what your expenses are and what other assets you have such as real estate, pensions, social security and other income. Surely you would be far better off than the person who didn't try and has savings worth $ 0, or worse yet is in debt for a large amount. Despite living in the land of opportunity, there are tens of millions of Americans who have savings and investments valued near zero. It's sad but true. But if your account has $700,000 in value what does that become if it doubles? BINGO!! It would then be worth $ 1.4 million, and you would be a millionaire. But if no $ 700,000, that would lead to no $ 1.4 million. To not begin your saving and investment account could be a million-dollar error. Don't be that guy or gal. Just getting started can build a small account that can grow into a fortune like a tiny acorn can grow into a giant oak tree. But with no acorn, no tree will grow. Plant that acorn.

One of the keys to wealth is to save money.

Having money saved enables you to take advantage of opportunities that come along without having to borrow and go into debt. I have invested in some stocks that have soared in price after I bought them. I was only able to buy them because money had been saved and was available to invest. Savings can protect your greatest wealth building tool, your income. Most "emergencies" can be fixed simply by writing a check if you have the money available (saved). And that could prevent you from borrowing when an emergency strikes.

On the next page is a graph of the stock Qualcomm (QCOM). The arrow shows when I bought the stock. It rose 2,500% over the next year or so. Over the next several years I was fortunate enough to do very well with other stocks (CREE, SMTC, EMC, APA, DVN, CHK and MTH come to mind among others). If you go to Google finance and look at their graphs (click on Max for time frame) you will see some very impressive rises between 1998 and 2008. But without savings I could not have bought any of them. Qualcomm was the very first stock I bought.

Beginner's luck but enabled by saving and reading about that company and others and realizing there was an opportunity there. For most investors individual stocks may be too volatile and may carry more risk (of loss) than is ideal. For most investors mutual funds will do the job nicely and with less risk.

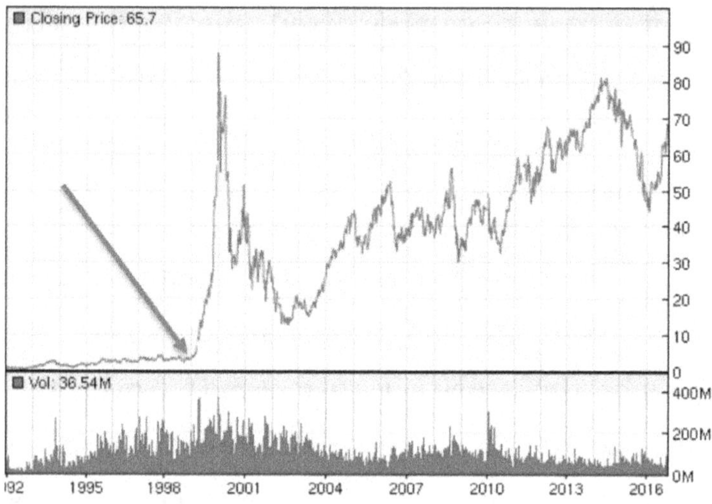

Each person decides for themselves how much they will save and invest. Let's take a look at what happens when a person saves. And contrast that with what happens if a person does not save. And for the sake of this example, we'll use a time frame of forty years, which is the length of a normal working life. We'll use a 12 percent rate of return for the illustration's sake. Not all investors will achieve a 12 percent rate of return, but it can be done. The overall stock market has averaged nearly 12% (11.8%) annual growth for the past 70 or more years. Many people have done that well and better. We believe that not only should each person save and invest but saving is one of the keys to becoming comfortable, financially independent or wealthy.

If a person averages only $40,000 per year over their work life, what amount would they amass over the forty years?

0 Percent Saved

If a person saves 0 percent, well, zero times anything (as you learned in elementary school) is zero. After forty years, this person would have $0. They would be broke. This is what is sometimes referred to as poverty. Poverty is often defined as a low income. Zero or a negative net worth would be another type of poverty. Twenty-five percent or more of senior citizens have done this. More people do this than you would believe.

Some people actually have little or no savings

but do have debts. They may therefore have a net worth of less than $ 0. It could actually be a negative number. I've read that the average American dies still owing $61,000 as debt.

1 Percent Saved

If they saved just 1 percent, that would be just $400 per year. Most people would say, "What's $400? Why even bother?" Well, $400 per year forty years later is $396,000. That would pay you an income of about $32,000 per year, which is $2,600 per month. This illustration assumes a withdrawal of 7.5 percent per year. That should be sustainable forever if the person is averaging 12 percent return. $2,600 per month is a fair amount of money. You would rather have such an income than not have it. In combination with other income, it could provide for a comfortable way of life. It is certainly far better than the zero percent example above, thus illustrating the value of saving.

And let's imagine you did that between the ages of 18 and 58. Let's say that that person begins taking out $2,600 per month. But the account continues to increase as it earns 12% per year. What would it be worth 20 years later at age 78? It would then be worth $1.715 million so even the person saving just 1% for 40 years would eventually become a millionaire but at an older age.

5 Percent Saved

If the person puts away 5 percent of their income, that would be $2,000 per year. That is less than $200 per month. **That will grow into an account worth $1,980,000 after 40 years.** That person would be rich and a millionaire. See, now wasn't that simple? And that account will kick out an income of $148,000 per year or about $12,377 per month forever! Not bad! It would be like winning a million-dollar lottery except that you can control this and actually do it. There are not odds of millions to one against you like there are in the lotteries. You might not do as well as these illustrations. But you might do even do better.

10 Percent Saved

If the person puts away 10 percent of

income, that would be $4,000 per year. That is only $333 per month and is doable for most people who work. They will build an account worth $3,960,806 (nearly $4 million). They will be a multi-millionaire. And remember, this is a person with a modest income. What if they earn more? What if they have two or three incomes in the family? Many families do.

This will produce an income of $297,000 per year or about $24,755 per month. Now ask yourself, "Could you enjoy your life with an income of $24,755 per month and with no need to go to work?" Most people would be fine with those circumstances. And the best thing is that you can make that happen.

See next page.

$40,000 Income Example

Percent saved yearly	Amount invested per year	Value after forty years	Payout per year at 7.5 percent	Income PER MONTH at 7.5 percent
0 percent	$0	$0	$0	$0
1 percent	$400	$396,000	$32,000	$2,600
5 percent	$2,000	$1,980,403	$148,000	$12,377
10 percent	$4,000	$3,960,806	$297,000	$24,755

Wow, that is pretty amazing! Just by saving each month, a person can become a millionaire and a multimillionaire at that. Nice. Once you understand that, why would anyone not save? One doesn't even need a huge income to do this. Compare the percent saved above with how much is taken by social security (12.4 percent). The government will "hold" your money for you. Of course, with social security, you really don't own anything. In your own saving and investment plan, you would own it all. In your own saving plan, you can use the money if you need to. In social security you cannot use the money at all except when they pay you benefits subject to their rules. With your own investments you own it and can leave it to your heirs. When you die in many cases your social security vanishes too. There are some survivor benefits from social security but nothing like your own investments, and your heirs may not qualify for any survivor benefits at all. That depends on ages and family relationships.

My advice is to save money. Pay yourself first. The first bill you pay each month should be to your own investment account. Should you fail to save, there is a good chance you will experience hardship. In fact, I just read today in the newspaper that about 33 percent of seniors have no savings for retirement. I've also read that 97% of 65-year olds cannot write a check for $600. Knowing this, don't let that happen to you.

Why do you need savings for retirement? Well, invested money can earn money or buy investments that grow wealth and sometimes can double your money a number of times. Money you have saved and invested will produce a flow of income to protect you from want or the need to work in order to produce income. It is income without the need to spend your time and energy working for it. And that's a great thing. At that point, you would be **financially independent.** You no longer need to work. Instead, you are free to do whatever you wish, or do nothing at all if that is what suits you. The reason people buy lottery tickets is to get a large payout to become financially independent. In truth, they could produce their own fortune simply by saving and investing. And keep in mind my young readers, at the ages of 65 or 70 most people have some aches and pains or health issues that could make working a painful and or more difficult endeavor, or even an impossibility.

Having invested wealth also protects you from unexpected or emergency expenses that could otherwise put you into debt and financial hardship. It also makes it more possible for you to do lots of other things that you enjoy doing. You can devote your time to whatever you wish. Things like travel, volunteering, or relaxing at the beach, or running through a park are things a person might enjoy when they have free time and the money to pay their expenses. Or they may just enjoy an afternoon nap. Or they may enjoy just poking around the house and relaxing.

The table below is similar, but in this case, we use the example of a higher income earning person or family. Again, the person who does not save at all produces a total value and income of zip, zero, nada, or nothing. So even though the income is bigger, the person could still end up broke, and many people do. This is more common than you think. And you don't want to go there.

$100,000 Income Example

Percent invested per year	Amount invested per year	Value after forty years	Payout per year at 7.5 %	Payout per month at 7.5 %
0 percent	$0	$0	$0	$0
1 percent	$1,000	$990,201	$74,265	$6,189
5 percent	$5,000	$4,951,008	$371,325	$30,943
10 percent	$10,000	$9,902,017	$742,651	$61,887

Wow, that's crazy. Are you saying that a person could amass $9.9 million and have an income of $742,651 per year? And that would break down to $61,887 per month? Per month! That is amazing! Isn't it? Can you imagine getting paid $61,887 per month? Sounds like fun to me! And those are figures that an ordinary person could actually do. I mean a person could earn $100,000 per year and more, especially in a two-income family. And a person could definitely save or invest $10,000 per year. In fact, that $10,000 might actually cost only $6,500 or $7,000 if the $10,000 was invested in a tax-deductible plan such as a 401(k), 403(b), or IRA. It could even cost only $5,000 to have $10,000 invested if company matching is available. And being tax deductible that $5,000 would cost even less, $4,000 in New York State. For $4,000 out of pocket that person could have $10,000 in their account **that year.** That would be an effective return of 150 % that first year.

But the other side of the coin is that the person could also choose to save 0 percent and have savings worth zero and an income of $0 per month and per year. In that case, the money earned over those forty years would be gone as would the forty years. The time will pass anyway. Why not use that time to build your fortune? Why not become a millionaire or rich instead of poor? And that's why I say, "Save money. Pay yourself first. The first bill you pay each month should be to your own investment account." And that will provide a rich future for you and your loved ones. And of course, the money you invest each month is very important because it is an investment that can grow and create a better future. It's different than the money you use to spend or pay bills where what you spend is gone forever.

Why would anyone choose to be poor instead of wealthy? Great question. Basically, most folks don't think about it. And that is the answer. If you don't think about it the money will flow away and disappear and be gone. You won't know where it went unless you become intentional and tell your dollars where to go and what to do.

Folks don't intend to become poor. But we all can intend to do better with our money. Usually schools fail to teach these simple but very practical ideas. But so what? You take the responsibility to learn these things because they are vital to creating a great future. In most cases, people simply don't understand how simple it is to choose to work and earn money to invest and how great the potential is for producing real wealth in the future. Ordinary folks can do this. And they do every day. This book will attempt to show some ways a person could make that better choice.

Another reason why people don't save the larger amounts is that they simply don't write a budget and tell their money where to go and what to do. If you don't tell it where to go, money will leave anyway. And may leave you penniless. Money flows which is why it's called currency. And like water flows downhill, money flows away unless told where to go and what to do. Writing it down on paper is an important step in directing your money where you want it to go. It is ideal to sit down with your spouse or partner or alone if single each month, go over your goals and write a budget to guide your spending for the month.

Advertising brainwashes people to believe they must have that new car and have it right now, even if you have to borrow to get it. Before you know it, your income is reduced or gone. Gone to pay the bills on your debts.

Save more than 10%, and you could produce similar results in an even shorter amount of time. Or earn more income and you could build a larger investment portfolio as well. When you save and invest more you speed up the process and can be richer at a younger age.

There is an old saying, "There is more than one way to skin an apple." And there are many ways to save and invest. The bottom line is that it can be done rather easily when you are intentional. The purpose of this book is to suggest some ways to do that and explain why you might want to. It is obvious why you would want to, right? We all want a better future.

Perhaps the easiest way to save and invest is to sign up for payroll deduction at your place of work. That way, the money is deposited into your investment account automatically before you receive your paycheck. That is total ease. The investments are on autopilot. You just watch it grow and suffer no temptation to spend the money because it isn't in your hands or wallet.

Even if you already have received your pay checks deposited in your checking account, it is simple to set up automatic deposits to your savings or investment accounts from your checking account.

That is pretty amazing! Just by saving each month, a person can become a millionaire and a multimillionaire at that. Nice. One doesn't even need a huge income to do this. Compare the percentages saved above with how much is taken by social security (12.4 percent). Everyone is required to contribute to social security. Of course, with social security, you really don't own anything. In the above program, you would own it all. And with social security, you have almost no say as to how much you receive each month. With your own personal account, you are in total control and can literally write your own check or move funds into your bank account with a few mouse clicks on your computer when you want to. With your own accounts you can also choose what to invest in. It is easy to do and may produce better returns than Social Security's record of very low annual returns.

My advice is to save money. Pay yourself

first. The first bill you pay each month should be to your own investment account. If you don't take care of your future, who do you think will do it for you? That's right, nobody will. Should you fail to save, there is a good chance you will experience hardship. Remember that 33 percent of seniors have no savings for their future or retirement. Don't let that happen to you.

Why do you need savings for retirement or to be financially independent and enjoy a rich life? I think that is obvious. Invested wealth can also earn money and can produce a cash flow or future income for you. Once you have built a large enough amount of investments, it will not be necessary to work to produce income. Some people might need $1 million. Another might need just $500,000 or a third person may want $3 million. It depends on how much you spend each month, the costs of your wants and needs, and factors such as other sources of income. Your choice is; you can work to produce income, or your investments can produce that income for you. The choice is yours.

A Fine Gift

Here is another cool example. Suppose your parents gave you a $5,000 graduation gift, wedding gift, or Bar Mitzvah gift, and you put that into an IRA or, better yet, a Roth IRA. You leave it there for forty years and never add to it. But you do manage it well and earn 18 percent per year. Granted an 18% return is uncommon but possible. What would it be worth? It would be worth $6,348,000 and would pay an income of $476,000 per year (if you take 7.5 percent each year), which is just under $40,000 per month. If in a Roth IRA that would be $40,000 tax-free! Very cool!

It might be rare to earn 18 percent per year. I would answer that you might do worse or better. But if you are going to dream, why not dream big. Nobody can know the future with certainty decades from now. But you might do even better than that. And you certainly won't do that well if you spend the gift or don't try to invest for long-term gain.

But what if the gift were five times as big or

ten times as big? If nobody gives you gifts such as that, what is stopping you from giving yourself that gift? That's right; nothing is stopping you. Do it.

Main point: A penny saved is a penny earned, goes the saying. But it can become much much more. John D Rockefeller was a saver. And his savings helped him start his wildly successful business. Giant fortunes grow from small beginnings.

CHAPTER 7: THE RULE OF 72

Did you know that Albert Einstein considered his discovery of the "rule of 72" to be his most important discovery? And he considered the magic of compound interest or earnings to be the 8th wonder of the world!

Use this rule to your advantage.

The rule of 72 is a good way to estimate what an investment will grow to be over time. It is one of the really important ideas about finance. If I were to ask you, "How much would you like as an allowance or retirement income?" Would you prefer $200,000 per month? Or would you prefer perhaps $133 per month? Or maybe you would prefer an income of $266 per month? Would that be a hard choice to make? And would you believe these wildly different amounts could result from the same amount invested and for the same amount of time? It is of course a silly question, because everyone would choose the $ 200,000 per month. They may not believe such an income is possible, yet it is. Many people make the wrong choice, choosing those smaller amounts as it often is not spelled out as clearly as in this book. Of course, it would not be a tough choice. But lots of people make the wrong choice. Most people do in fact. Many of them are directed toward those smaller figures by financial salesmen who sell them products that are not the best. In fact, they are terrible products. Many people actually chose the lower numbers because the products that earn the smaller incomes they are told are considered to be "safer." Hmmmm, that is very interesting. It is also very wrong headed. Our schools could teach how numbers and money work together. The information is available to anyone who seeks it. It's not secret. But each of us is responsible to become informed. And if we don't then shame on us. These ideas are of great importance because money and wealth have a huge impact on every aspect of our lives.

Oddly enough, all three of the above figures resulted from the same amount of money invested for the same length of time. Could different rates of return result in such huge differences in income? Simply put, YES!

The rule of 72 is a well-known idea. Yet most people have never heard of it. It is very important though. Many financial professionals know of it. And unfortunately, many financial professionals actually sell the products that result in the lower numbers above.

Let me explain how the rule of 72 works. If you take the number 72 and divide into that number, the annual rate of return on your investment, the answer is the number of years it takes for your investment to double. Doubling your investment is very profitable. People like to do that. Here are some investment returns. You can achieve any of these: 2 percent per year; 4 percent per year; 8 percent per year; 12 percent per year; 18 percent per year; and for a superstar, 24 percent per year.

Rate of return refers to how much you earn on your investment PER YEAR. Percent means per 100. A 6% return means you would earn $6 per $100 invested per year. If you invested $200 you would earn $12. If you invested $10,000 you would earn $600, $6 for each $100.

For this illustration, why don't we begin with an investment of $10,000 that we leave for a period of thirty-six years. That will illustrate both the rule of 72 and the effect of these rates of return. We will see the result of these differing rates of return. Most people would find it difficult to leave $10,000 invested for 36 years. That is why we each need to have self discipline, and intentionally tell our money where to go and how to be invested. To do that we need to have patience as lots of time needs to pass to double our investment a number of times. This is just an exercise. We're doing this to show how important your rate of return is to your future financial well being.

2 Percent Return (Per Year)

If you invested $10,000 for thirty-six years at 2 percent, well, two divided into seventy-two goes thirty-six times. It would take thirty-six years to double your investment. Your $10,000 would double **just once** to $20,000, which could produce an income of $1,600 per year or about $133 per month. That is taking 8 percent per year as income.

And since 8 percent is greater than 2 percent, the money would eventually all be gone. That would take a bit over fourteen years.

4 Percent Return

At 4 percent, four divided into seventy-two goes eighteen times. Your investment would double in eighteen years, meaning it would double twice in thirty-six years. So your $10,000 would double twice.

It would go

$10,000 -> $20,000 -> $40,000

Your $40,000 would provide $3,200 per year at 8 percent or about $266 per month. Very interesting. In this case, the money would be all gone in 17.4 years.

8 Percent

At 8 percent, eight divided into seventy-two goes nine times. Your investment would double in nine years. It would **double four times** in thirty-six years. The 8 percent is a return you might get from bonds or mutual funds. The lower 2 percent and 4 percent might be obtained though bank accounts and insurance policies. At 8 percent, it would double four times and it would double as follows.

$10,000-> $20,000-> $40,000 -> $80,000 -> $160,000

That $160,000 would pay you about $12,800 per year or about $1,000 per month. That figure seems similar to what a person might receive from social security. Of course, with social security, you put in way more than $10,000. Which illustrates that social security is an expensive "investment." But $1,000 per month is a nice amount of money. We would all enjoy receiving $1,000 per month. Of course, in AD 2047, it won't be worth then what it is today. It will not buy in 2047 what it would buy today.

If your investments earn 8 percent and you withdraw 8 percent, the account will never run out of money.

12 Percent Return

Investments that might return 12% would include equity investments such as stocks, mutual funds and other ownership investments. Your account would double faster and more times because the value would double every six years.

<u>Twelve</u> divided into seventy-two goes six times. Your investment would double in six years. Which would mean that that $10,000 would double six times in thirty-six years. It would double as follows.

$10,000->$20,000->$40,000->$80,000->$160,000->$320,000->$640,000

Starting amount	$10,000
1 double	$ 20,000
2 doubles	$ 40,000
3 doubles	$ 80,000
4 doubles	$ 160,000
5 doubles	$ 320,000
6 doubles	$ 640,000

That $640,000 would pay an income of $51,200 or about

$4,267 per month. This is a nice sum. That is a lot more than the $266 per month. And that $640,000 would have grown from just $10,000 with no additional contributions, which is **amazing!**

In this case, the account would grow in value despite withdrawals because 12 percent is greater than the 8 percent that is being withdrawn. In fact, twenty years later it would be worth $2,707,870, **despite taking out $4,267 per month!** Wow, that is very cool!

And what you need to understand is that this is the result of the same amount of money invested for the same amount of time. It doubles faster and more times. It would result in a bigger total and therefore a larger income. It's just a better situation all around. Wouldn't you agree?

18 Percent Return

The next percent we'll look at is 18 percent. Can you actually do that? You would have to be a pretty successful investor to do that. Most people don't do that well. But it can be done. I've done it myself.

Well, eighteen divided into seventy-two goes four times. Therefore, your money would double every four years. That means that in thirty-six years, it would double nine times. **At 18% return the $10,000 would double nine times in thirty-six years.**

Nine doubles!

$10,000->$20,000->$40,000->$80,000->$160,000->$320,000-> $640,000

It would continue for three more doubles.

$640,000->$1,280,000->$2,560,000 -> $5,120,000

See table on next page.

Doubles	Starting value $ 10,000
1 double	$20,000
2 doubles	$40,000
3 doubles	$80,000
4 doubles	$ 160,000
5 doubles	$ 320,000
6 doubles	$ 640,000
7 doubles	$ 1,280,000
8 doubles	$ 2,560,000
9 doubles	$ 5,120,000

The above is a great result but would take lots of time (36 years), and good fortune in investing.

$5,120,000 is a nice amount of money or wealth. This person would be a multimillionaire. That $5,120,000 would produce an income of $409,600 per year without any need to work. You would definitely be financially independent. Meaning, you would be independent of working to produce income. **That income would be about $34,000 per month.** That is a princely sum. Most people would be very happy to have that amount of monthly income. I know I would be.

Again, this account would continue to grow because the 18 percent growth is greater than the 8 percent withdrawn. This account will eventually be worth millions and tens of millions in the future. In 20 years (after that 36-year period) despite taking out $34,000 per month, that account would be worth **$103 million!!** With that amount of wealth, you would have lots and lots of options.

24 Percent Return

Now the final rate of return I will write about is 24 percent. Is that actually doable? And the answer is yes. Peter Lynch who ran Magellan fund had a rate of return in excess of 30 percent as did his predecessor. It's been done. There was actually an ordinary woman, who was an auditor for the IRS, who saw that people who invested in stock sometimes had very large portfolios and tended to be wealthy so she became a stock investor and over a certain number of years she had a rate of return of 23 or 24 percent. It's a very famous story and I'll tell you a bit more about it later in this chapter.

Warren Buffet is famous for achieving a rate of return on the order of 24% per year. People who have invested with him have huge net worths and are quite happy. He is one of the richest men in America with a net worth approaching or exceeding $60 Billion dollars!

Twenty-four divided into seventy-two goes three times. This means that your investment would double every three years. It would double twelve times in thirty-six years. Let's pick it up where it is after doubling nine times and double it three more times for a total of twelve times or <u>twelve doubles</u>!

$5,120,000 -> $10,240,000 -> $20,480,000 -> $40,960,000 Wow! That is a ton of money!

Wow, $10,000 invested for thirty-six years, if you were fortunate enough to get a return of 24 percent, you would have about $41 million. That is really a staggering sum. **That would pay you about $3,276,800 per year or about $273,000 per month. Crazy but TRUE!** And you would be leaving $40 million to your "happy" heirs or enjoy it as would suit you.

The question to you is "Would you prefer to have the income of $273,000 per month or would you prefer the $266 per month?" Well, it's no contest. These are numbers that are real and actually do happen. One of the sad facts is that many Americans choose the investments that pay them the $266 per month not because they want the smaller amount, but because they are unaware of the consequences of the rule of 72 and how it works. And of course, lots of people don't ever save the $10,000 making their monthly payout $0.

Chapter Postscript:

The rule of 72 is an excellent way to estimate a future total. It isn't accurate to the penny, but it is a good ballpark figure. For example, if we calculate the actual value of the last example, we would get the following:

If $10,000 were invested at 24 percent for thirty-six years, the final total would be $51,900,000 (Wow!) rather than the rule of 72 estimate of $41,000,000. In either case, you would be a happy investor and a person without financial concerns.

You can calculate these numbers easily and accurately using any financial calculator or financial calculator App on your smart phone.

The Story of the Lady from the IRS

This is a great story. It seems that this person, when she died, left an estate in the order of $23 or $24 million despite the fact that she never earned a lot of money by way of income. Well, it seems that as an auditor for the IRS, she observed that those people who owned stocks (the so-called riskiest investments) often had large amounts of wealth. She also observed that those people who had a great deal of money owned stocks. She became a stock investor and invested with Merrill Lynch, and over her lifetime, she became a very successful stock investor. She was so successful that when she died, she left an estate valued at about $24 million. I believe she had a rate of return of about 24 percent, thus demonstrating what the average person can do. It's a remarkable story. And one final point: when she died, she was collecting $1 million dollars a year just in dividends from her stock investments. That is about $20,000 per week. That is fantastic! Just goes to show you what you or any other person can do.

What $ 10,000 becomes after 36 years:

Annual Rate of Return	Total after 36 years	Income from that amount at 5% payout
4%	$ 42,106	$ 2,105 / year
8%	$ 176,448	$ 8,822 / year
12%	$ 735,925	$ 36,796 / year
18%	$ 6,213,413	$ 310,671 / year
24%	$ 51,912,769	$ 2,595,638 / year

What might happen as wealth compounds over longer time periods?

If a person invests $4,000 per year and obtains 12% rate of return:

Time period.	Total Value
10 years	$77,369
20 years	$332,716
30 years	$1,175,000
40 years	$3,957,000
50 years	$13,136,000
60 years	$43,433,000
70 years	$143,423,000
80 years	$473,928,000

Are you kidding?

It is common for people to say, "But you can't get 12% return." Of course, they are wrong. The stock market in total has averaged about 12% for the last 80 years. You may do better or worse. Below are the returns of mutual funds my family owns. I'll show the ticker symbol, return for year to date (ytd), and average annual return since the founding of the fund and the year founded. See the table below. The table below was created on August 2, 2019 based on figures as of July 31,2019. Very current. See table below.

Fund Ticker	Return (ytd) JUST 7 MONTHS	Return for life of fund PER YEAR	SINCE
FOCPX	24.32%	13.76%	1984
FSPHX	13.56%	15.58%	1981
FSMEX	19.63%	14.73%	1998
FBALX	15.35%	9.23%	1986
FEQIX	15.67%	11.21%	1966
FCPGX	27.12%	11.9%	2004
FNCMX	22.99%	10.81%	2003
FBSOX	37.77%	13.7%	1998
FSCSX	27.99%	16.16%	1985
FSPTX	30.85%	13.02%	1981

Main point: Understand the Rule of 72 and why you want to seek those higher rates of return.

Given the returns shown above, what would $10,000 become if left there since the founding of the funds?

$10,000 left in FSPHX SINCE 1981 is today worth $3,680,000.

$10,000 left in FOCPX since 1984 is now worth $1,178,502.

$10,000 left in FEQIX since 1966 is today worth $3,503,000.

I know all three of the above involve a lot of time, but in each case the result is a millionaire and a financially secure person or family. And all for an investment of just $10,000.

CHAPTER 8: INVEST IN A TAX PROTECTED PLAN

The government will help you save for retirement or financial independence. Of course, they expect to share your profits too. That is fair and works for you anyway.

The next step is to invest in a tax-protected plan such as an IRA, a Roth IRA, a 401(k), a 403(b), or another tax-protected plan. Getting a good education, earning a good income, and saving are very important. But it is also important to learn about, understand and pay attention to taxes and how they can affect your money and investments. It was once said, "The power to tax is the power to destroy." That said, it is very wise to pay attention to taxes and have the rules work for you and not against you. If you don't pay attention, they can work against you and damage your financial future.

Numbers can sometimes be boring. But when those numbers are about your money, investments or wealth, they will not be boring. In fact, they may be very exciting and up lifting. The concepts discussed in this chapter are a key to your future success. And you may want to read this section several times. The numbers that I give are real numbers. They are not make-believe. This is not Fantasy Island. These are things that can and do happen. Most importantly, you can do these things.

Let's say that a person puts away $10,000 and they are fortunate and earn a return of 18 percent and they leave that money there for thirty-six years. Now everybody wants to do that, right? Put away $10,000 and not touch it for thirty-six years. Well, there is a huge payoff. That $10,000 would grow to over $6 million. That would produce an income of $497,000 per year or about $41,000 per month. That is remarkable. And that comes from an investment of just $10,000 that was just left alone there to percolate and grow over that period of time. That is pretty remarkable. And that $41,000-per-month income would be about $28,000 after taxes if you had to pay taxes on it. And we'll show you a way later with which you won't have to pay taxes on any of that income.

If instead a person invested $10,000 in a

plan that was not a tax-protected plan and got the same 18 percent return but had to pay taxes of 35 percent on the gain each year, the 18 percent would be an effective return of "only" 11.7 percent. And the value of the account would be "only" $661,000 and would pay an income of about $53,000 per year or about $4,400 per month.

The question you want to ask yourself is "Would you rather have $6 million dollars or would you rather have $661,000 dollars?" (For the very same investment.) I know which one I would rather have. And would you rather have a monthly income of $41,000 per month or would you rather have an income of $4,400 per month? Well, that's a pretty easy and obvious question to answer.

But most people don't do that. Most people don't put away a sum and never add another penny to it over time. Let's suppose that a person put away $10,000 and then put in another $333 per month, which is about $4,000 per year, over that time span. This is slightly less than a person can put into an IRA at this time ($ 6,000 per year). This would grow to be $20,191,565. Wow, that is incredible! This would produce an income of $1,600,000 per year or about $134,000 per month. After taxes, that would come out to be about $87,000 per month to live and enjoy your life. That is pretty remarkable, considering that these are doable numbers. A person could start with $10,000. A person could leave it there. And a person could contribute $333 per month and let the time pass and do the work. That is pretty remarkable.

Of course, getting an 18 percent return could be a challenge. While we give these examples as illustrations of what could happen, keep in mind that people have done that well (including the author) and better. It helps a great deal if you are a student of investing and read and learn about investing. There are lots of good sources that you can find in your public library or online or you could subscribe to. Investor's Business Daily (IBD) is an example of one fine source of information. Investors Business Daily is now a WEEKLY publication and an on line publication. Fidelity has a website that offers excellent information and is a fine company to invest with as well. There are lots of other excellent sources and mutual fund companies to invest with. Some are Vanguard, American Funds, T. Rowe Price and many others.

Here is another example of why tax-protected plans (also called tax-qualified plans) are such a great, great thing. And by the way, there are a number of such plans. There are IRA accounts, Roth IRA accounts, 401(k) if you work for a business, 403(b) if you work for a school system or hospital, and SIMPLE IRA accounts for self-employed. And there are a number of other types as well.

Here is another example. Suppose a person were to put $4,000 away per year starting with zero and earn 12 percent per year on average. After forty years . . . I know what you are thinking, "It's great to be a millionaire, but who wants to be sixty?" I understand that. But this will take care of the latter part of your life if you don't become a mega-millionaire at a young age, and most people don't. So just in case, you might want to consider this. About $4,000 per year would grow to be $3.9 million, which would produce an income of $317,000 per year or about $26,000 per month. After taxes, that would be about $17,000 per month. That is a pretty good outcome. Most people don't do that well, but it could be done. It is doable. And if I were a young person, I'd be starting that program like yesterday.

Sometimes people wait, and they don't make the saving a priority. Well, $4,000 per year for forty years would grow to be $3.9 million dollars. Let's say $4 million dollars. If that person waits ten years to begin, they invest for thirty years, what would that become? It would become $1.2 million dollars and would pay an income of $94,000 per year or about $7,800 per month. After taxes, that would be $5,100 per month. The questions you might want to ask yourself are the following:

Would you rather have $4 million dollars, or would you rather have $1.2 million dollars? I think most people would take the $4 million. And the moral of the story is "Get started right away."

And would you rather retire with an income of $5,100 net cash per month or would you rather have an income of $17,000 net cash (after taxes) each month?

It's amazing but true that by starting ten years sooner, you add $12,000 a month to your income. That is unbelievable! But like most people, suppose the person waited twenty years to begin that program. So instead of saving for forty years, they save for twenty years. Investing the same $4,000 per year, that would grow to only $332,000 and would pay an income of just $27,000 per year or $2,200 per month, which would be about $1,440 per month after taxes. And those are interesting examples.

But if you look at the first example. That by starting with $10,000 and putting roughly $300 a month in over your working lifetime, *you* could retire from work with nearly $7 million and an income of $46,000 per month. That is unbelievable to most people. And yet that could be done.

As you look at the examples above you notice that they are huge numbers and they do get reduced significantly by income taxes that have to be paid. You may be thinking, "who cares"? If I'm making $41,000 per month, I can afford to pay taxes of $16,000 per month. That is a big number and the moral of the story is that we should always be aware of taxes and pay attention to them. They can be a big deal.

What prevents many people from funding such an investment account is that they have debts to be paid first, leaving little or no money to invest. Debt can be and is a big obstacle for many people. Hopefully you will have none and therefore no reason to be concerned with debt. But most people have too much.

In the next section, we'll show you how you could do similar things except that with a Roth IRA, the income you produce will be totally tax-free for life.

Really? That would be wonderful.

Use the tax laws to help build your fortune.

CHAPTER 9: INVEST IN A ROTH IRA

This is all yours to keep. Any taxes were prepaid years ago. That's a beautiful thing.

And wouldn't it be nice to kick the IRS to the curb and eliminate tax bills. This chapter explains how to do that. And it is very easy to do.

Thank you, Senator Roth.

We understand that everybody enjoys paying taxes. What could be more fun than writing a $20,000 check to the IRS or other tax-collecting body? Well, not exactly. In fact, you may be fortunate and build a large portfolio that pays you hundreds of thousands of dollars each year. With such large payouts to you, there may also be large tax bills. Picture yourself having a tax bill to pay of $20,000 or $30,000, $40,000, or even $200,000. Do you think that would be great fun? Do you think you might have other things you could spend that money on that you might enjoy more? Could be.

A number of years ago, a Senator Roth sponsored a bill to encourage retirement savings.

This bill produced what is called the "Roth IRA." This is a great, great invention, particularly for young people. It is also beneficial to all people. What it features is that you can contribute to your IRA account, but you can designate it to be a Roth IRA. With a Roth IRA, you give up the tax deductibility of your contributions, but at the end of your career, all the income that this account produces is tax-free! That offers tremendous, tremendous benefits. It's a great, great investment vehicle. I wish they had it when I was a young person. You should definitely take advantage of it because it is available to you today. But let's give you a couple of examples to show how it works. And keep in mind that most of your portfolio, perhaps 90% will be growth which would mean avoiding taxes on 90% of your portfolio.

Suppose for example a person was to contribute $4,000 per year to a Roth IRA starting at age twenty. And they do that for just five years, and then they stop and never add another penny to it. If we assume a return of 12 percent, they would have accumulated about $27,000 after five years. And then just by letting thirty-five years pass and never touching that money or adding to it, at age sixty, after a total of forty years, that would be worth a total of $1.8 million. It's amazing to think that you could invest just $20,000 and then have a portfolio worth $1.8 million down the line. This could produce an income of $144,000 per year or about $12,000 per month. But what is special about the Roth IRA is that those $12,000 per month are totally tax-free, forever! It would not be reduced by taxes. That is a great, great thing! And most people could do that.

If taxed at 35 percent instead of the $12,000, you would have only $7,800. Ask yourself, would you rather have $12,000 or $7,800 to spend each month? Making your choice a Roth IRA would result in the higher figure.

But what would happen if instead of stopping after just five years, you were to save ($4,000 to $5,000) every year for the entire forty years? Your portfolio would be worth $3,960,800 dollars. That would produce an income of about $317,000 per year or about $26,000 per month.

Taxes on that same $317,000 would be about $100,000 if it were taxable. But with the

Roth IRA, there would be no taxes. This would save you about $100,000 per year. Or put another way, it would leave that $100,000 in your hands where you could use it as you wish.

And what might you do with that $100,000 per year? You might pay for a child's or grandchild's college education. You might start a business or invest in a business. You might contribute to a good cause or charity close to your heart. You might live in a better home or neighborhood. The possibilities are endless.

The examples we gave in the last chapter showed examples that paid an income of $46,000 and $26,000 per month. Well, if that were invested inside a Roth IRA, that would be $46,000 per month tax-free. So instead of having just $30,000 to keep and a $15,000 TAX BILL, you would have the entire $46,000 to keep and spend as you wish. It's truly an amazing thing.

Our advice would be to definitely save money. Pay yourself first. Begin your investments at as early an age as possible. Invest in an IRA or other tax-protected plan. And when you are choosing an IRA, choose a Roth IRA when possible because the tax benefits are fantastic!

Main point: If you reduce your future tax bills you will be glad you did. The Roth IRA is a great way to do that.

CHAPTER 10: DEFENSE WINS CHAMPIONSHIPS

Life happens. Be prepared.

Don't just build it. Protect it against loss as well.

Now that you have built this fortune through saving and investing, what steps should you follow to protect it? Great question. We know from Murphy's law that "What can go wrong, will go wrong." We understand there are threats and very damaging events that we may want to protect against.

Your greatest wealth building tool is your income. And yet you could lose that in a moment. One mistake while driving a car could result in a disabling accident making it impossible to continue working and earning an income. And it need not be your mistake. You could be struck by another driver who dozed off, is drunk, is distracted, or who's breaks fail, or who just got disoriented. It is very wise to drive a little slower. Never rush and stay alert and drive defensively. That means not depending on other people to not crash into you. You don't put your car where that could happen. I like the saying, "Whether you drive fast or slow, you arrive at the same destination." Arriving safe is the goal.

What could happen that could upset the apple cart or destroy your wealth or injure your family and your dreams? Here is a list of some possible hazards:

1. You could die. In fact, we all will some day.

2. You could become disabled. We are told that more people become disabled than die. How is that possible? Actually, it is if you think about it. A person can become disabled several times, but death happens only once.

3. You could have accidents of several types. Car accidents are probably the most common and deadly.

4. You could get sued. In fact, the wealthier you become the more likely you will be.

5. You could become sick with some dread disease and run up huge medical bills. Read my ebook "<u>LOSE WEIGHT EASILY</u>" for ideas about preventing cancer and cardiovascular diseases. They are two of the deadliest and most costly diseases. And

they are both preventable for the most part. My estimate is 95% are preventable for cardiovascular and 50% are preventable for cancer.

6. And I'm sure there are a few others I'm not aware of at this moment. Sharks? Bears? Lightning? And many more.

So how do we best deal with these risks that could ruin our plans and impoverish us and our families? Let's take each one at a time.

It is wise to buy insurance that insures the income in the event of any loss of income.

When a person dies their income typically ends. There are exceptions like Elvis Presley was earning $40 million per year years after he passed. But for most people death means the end of income, so it is wise to insure that income against loss. A person can buy **life insurance** to pay off should that person die. What is being insured is really the person's income. The income may be vital for the surviving family members. That could provide the funds to replace the lost income so that surviving children and other dependents are provided for. The life insurance should be term insurance and would ideally pay 10 to 12 times the annual income of the person who died. Life insurance should never have a saving component attached. Savings and investments should be held separately.

A person could suffer a disabling injury or illness. A disability could also end the person's income and disabilities are fairly common. Like life insurance it is wise to purchase disability insurance to protect your loved ones against loss of income due to disability. There are various kinds of policies, so it is important that you become a student and seek to learn a bit about the subject. It would also be wise to discuss your questions with a financial professional. After you have learned a bit about these two insurances and have purchased the necessary policies, you can cross those two risks off your list because they are gone. You have paid the insurance company to accept that risk instead of you having the risk yourself. Sweet.

Of course, you will need automobile insurance, health insurance and possibly an umbrella liability policy if you might get sued (like if you have money or assets that could attract lawyers and people who would love to sue and get some of your money). Study and learn about these topics too. Talk to experts. Remember that an ounce of prevention is worth a pound of cure. With insurance you prevent the loss even if the event were to happen. You might not be able to prevent the death, disability or injury but you can prevent the financial harm that can result simply by buying the insurance.

It will be to your advantage. By paying premiums that are often inexpensive you can eliminate these hazards that if left uninsured could wipe out your investments and financial well being in a single event, illness or accident. Your peace of mind and financial security demand that you consider these wise protections.

Main point: Life happens and so do risks of great loss. Insurance can often protect you.

CHAPTER 11: PHYSICAL FITNESS

You can feel great and be strong. Or you can be weak and feel poorly. Easy choice.

A sound mind in a sound body.

At first glance, you might say, "What does physical fitness have to do with becoming rich or a millionaire?" That is a very logical question. There are two parts to the answer. First, you may have noticed that a number of plans in this book take time to accomplish. And in some cases, can take lots of time. Well, since you only get one body, it would be wise to take good care of it so that it lasts a very long time. When it wears out, so do you. The second part of the answer is that this book is about more than just numbers. Becoming financially independent is to enhance your enjoyment of your life. Being physically fit will better help you to live to a ripe old age. And it will make it possible for you to enjoy your entire life more for a number of reasons as I will explain.

Excellent physical fitness will help you do the following:

1. Live longer and feel good.

2. Increase your ability to do things you otherwise could not do.

3. Increase your personal safety.

4. Better enable you to meet emergencies, and more.

5. Be here alive and feeling well to enjoy your financial success.

In this chapter we want to talk about physical fitness. Physical fitness is one of the keys to enjoying a long and happy life. I'd like to take a moment and look at how we developed as creatures over the last one or two million years. During that time, we basically walked wherever we went. There were no other means of transportation. We occasionally ran either to escape from danger or perhaps in pursuit of hunting prey. Perhaps people ran during warfare times, to escape danger or even for play and recreation. In addition, during that time, there was no soda or other junk foods such as candy. So basically, when we were thirsty we drank water, and when hungry you would eat fruits, berries, or game. Those food items would be rich in vitamins and minerals unlike junk or processed foods. That gives you a clue that water may be the best drink for us. And that exercise such as walking is part of what we do in order to stay strong and healthy. While living in a modern society, it often isn't necessary to do exercise, yet our bodies still demand it and benefits from it. It makes sense that our body would benefit from doing exercise on a regular basis such as walking and probably drinking water as our beverage of choice. Exercise keeps our body working well. It keeps us strong and prepared to meet emergencies or danger. When people cannot exercise or move due to accident or illness, their bodies break down and weaken fairly quickly.

If you want to enjoy your life, it is absolutely essential that you be physically fit. It's not too hard to do. In fact, it can be a very enjoyable enterprise because you can exercise by playing a sport or game that you love and enjoy. And there are many, many benefits. When you are fit you look better, and you have greater abilities because you are stronger. You have greater endurance. You become injured less often. You will be safer because when you are strong, fewer people will seek to victimize you. You enjoy better health. Exercise has been shown to reduce your likelihood of suffering from cardiovascular disease and cancers which are the number one and number two causes of death in America. Likewise, exercise has been shown to prevent and cure type 2 diabetes. Diabetes is a common cause of death and the number one cause of blindness and amputations. And there are numerous other benefits that flow from keeping yourself physically fit, strong, and healthy. Once fit, you will enjoy the probability of greater longevity. If you live an additional ten or twenty years, your investments can double a couple of times more, making you perhaps four times as wealthy. So it's a win-win-win situation. We encourage everyone to be as physically fit as they would like to be. Here are several types of fitness.

There are a number of different kinds of fitness. I'll name just five of them and will say a few words about each kind.

They are the following:

1. Aerobic fitness

2. Strength fitness

3. Flexibility

4. Endurance

5. Skill

Let's take a look at each type.

Aerobic Fitness

One type of fitness is aerobic fitness. Aerobic fitness produces what is known as the training effect. Aerobic exercises are those that cause you to breathe faster and your heart beat faster and last longer than ten minutes. They cause a dramatic increase in your heart rate. And those things go to produce the training effect. That training effect changes your body over time so that oxygen is quickly brought to your muscles preventing fatigue and enabling you to perform for hours. Aerobic means with air. And oxygen is essential for our muscles to work or even live. Aerobic exercises would include these: running, walking (at a brisk pace), basketball, soccer, swimming (at a brisk pace), bicycling, vigorous dance classes, or aerobics classes. Aerobic exercises would also include using machines at gyms such as treadmills or stair masters or exercise cycles. All these can cause you to work at a high level and in excess of ten minutes, so they will produce the training effect. So workout and enjoy yourself! I was very blessed to be a teacher by profession. That enabled me to have a schedule like a school child. I could then come home from school and go out and play just like a child. In my case I'd go off for a six or eight mile run. I just loved it. One of my favorites was an 8 mile loop that came back to our home after running across the top of the Kensico dam in Valhalla, New York. Or I might run a similar distance on the horse trails in the Rockefeller Preserve in Sleepy Hollow, New York and imagine John D Rockefeller walking on those very same trails. They are lovely wooded trails, now a state park, but still used by the Rockefellers to this day. It was recreation, play and fitness all rolled into one activity.

The training effect was measured and quantified by Dr. Kenneth Cooper in his famous book <u>Aerobics.</u> In fact, the word aerobics used commonly in our language today comes from his research and that book. That book is also given the credit for starting the running boom, which began in the 1970s. From the first New York City Marathon, which happened in 1970 where there were 127 runners, it has grown to a race with in excess of 40,000 participants today. And many more seek to get into the race, but not all can get in. People love to be fit and to train. Once fit, few people wish to become unfit. Being fit simply feels great! When I'm fit, which is most of the time over the past 50 years there is nothing I would rather do then go into Rockefeller State Park and run 8 miles or so on the hilly horse trails. It is not always easy but is always a great thing and makes for a great day.

Dr. Cooper went so far as to say that if you didn't have aerobic fitness, you were not fit. Even if you had big strong muscles, you would probably tire very quickly if you didn't also have aerobic fitness in addition to those big strong muscles.

Aerobic fitness is phenomenal because it enables you to do two or three things at the same time. For example, I love running. And I love swimming. So when I'm exercising, I'm also doing something that I love doing. I'm also developing aerobic fitness and getting all the benefits of that training effect. At the same time, I'm also strengthening the muscles involved in that exercise, keeping extra weight off, enjoying the outdoors, and more.

Some of the training effects that Dr. Cooper described in his book include these. The size of the lungs will increase through use to supply the oxygen your body demands. And the increased lung size helps accomplish that. The blood vessels grow in size and number. This enables your body to deliver oxygen to the muscles, which prevents them and you from fatiguing. Those same blood vessels also remove metabolic waste products, preventing fatigue. In addition to preventing fatigue, this helps lower your blood pressure and helps prevent serious problems such as strokes and heart attacks. When you do aerobic exercise, you burn fuel, which helps reduce your weight, and that too helps prevent cardiovascular diseases such as heart attacks and strokes. Keeping your weight within normal range also helps prevent type 2 Diabetes. There are many benefits.

Another training effect is that your resting pulse rate will slow. A highly trained athlete can have a resting pulse in the order of forty beats per minute. And when I was training for marathon races (26.2 miles) and running up to eighty miles per week, my resting pulse was about forty beats per minute. Because I still love exercise and work out every day, my resting pulse is still close to that today (I'm age seventy three). And the other night in bed, my resting pulse was thirty-five. Incredible! Normal is seventy-two, so it's good to know I'm not normal. It's fun to be weird. Note: a lower rate is better. It is good for you to have a strong healthy heart, and large easy flow blood vessels, obviously. We only get one heart and it is essential to living and being well. What would be the point of building wealth if you didn't also have great health to enjoy it with. Aerobic exercises help us keep it working well and helps us feel great.

The lower heart rate is because the heart is stronger and can pump more blood with each heartbeat, and the blood vessels are larger and can pass the blood more quickly and easily. This also results in lower blood pressure. And there are more changes that are part of the training effect. For example, Training produces stronger muscles because they are exercised in doing the aerobic exercises. Runners, soccer players, basketball players have strong legs for example.

In addition to the physical benefits of aerobic exercises, there is a great fun factor. You can choose a form of exercise that is fun for you and have a blast. You can do it with friends. You can make new friends while sharing an activity, while achieving goals, and while forming great memories that will last a lifetime. If there were one type of exercise that you were limited to doing and you were only able to do one type of exercise, it should be aerobic exercise. That will protect your health and give you many other benefits, all at the same time.

In addition to the training effect, aerobic exercisers also develop specific strength of the muscles used in those exercises. Swimmers will have strong muscles in their back, arms, and shoulders. Runners and cyclists will have strong legs as we just said.

There are also emotional benefits. The so–called runners' high is a feeling of euphoria and wellbeing that happens during and following such workouts. Aerobic exercises and training is also a great and positive way to deal with emotional stresses, fears, anxiety, and other negative emotions. Training often just eliminates those emotions altogether. It also feels good to be fit and not tire easily, to look good, to accomplish goals and to be making progress. All these things contribute to an attitude of optimism and a positive mental attitude. These are some of the reasons why aerobic exercises are my number one choice.

We also mentioned earlier that the fourth type of fitness is endurance. Well, endurance is just the result of doing aerobic exercises and getting the training effects. If you run for an hour, or you swim for an hour, or if you build up so you can run for two hours, or you run marathons, you will have developed and enjoy tremendous endurance as well as great satisfaction for accomplishing those goals or milestones. As a matter of fact, endurance comes directly from doing aerobic training.

Strength

Another form of fitness is what I would call strength. Strength is always good to have. It's never a bad thing. Strength enables you to do things you otherwise would not be able to do. It protects you in a number of ways. Where does it come from? Strength results from doing exercise against resistance where force needs to be applied to overcome that resistance. As muscles need to work to overcome resistance, they grow in size and strength. Some exercises that offer resistance would be things like lifting weights. Training with weights will cause your muscles to grow in size and strength over time. Your body weight is something you always have with you. And that enables you to do some of my favorite exercises, which work against the force of gravity on your body weight. I like to do push-ups and pull-ups. As a matter of fact, just doing those two exercises for a few minutes a day will enable you to strengthen many muscles all at the same time. They will strengthen your whole upper body: your arms, shoulders, chest, and back all at the same time, with just two simple exercises. It is easy to note improving strength as your number of repetitions increase, and the exercises become easier as you become stronger. And improvement can happen quickly. Here, the resistance and weight you use is the weight of your body.

Another device that is outstanding at increasing strength is the Bowflex. It is simple to use, enjoyable, and very effective. There are many and varied strength building machines found at most gyms.

A lot of people belong to gyms and sports clubs. Machines at gyms offer many opportunities to work against resistance. Of course, there are weights such as barbells and dumbbells. There are also machines such as "Stair Masters", "Gravitrons", treadmills, Nautilus, elliptical trainers, and many more kinds. They offer you many ways to strengthen muscles. You can focus on any part of your body that you want to strengthen.

One of your best investments would be to buy a quality pair of running shoes and some high quality socks. We have to keep our feet comfy. A pair of quality running shoes coupled with the desire to train is often all you need. Money spent or invested in a gym membership is an investment in better health, fitness and longevity. And gyms offer many ways to have FUN as well.

Strength protects you. It shows visibly from the size and bulging of toned muscles. Predators see that and will usually leave you alone, preferring weaker victims. Being fit I've often been asked, "Are you military?" And "Are you former police?" Well bad guys size you up too without you noticing and when you appear fit and strong will leave you alone. You could also travel with a big friend. That works too.

So that makes two types of fitness we've talked about. Aerobic fitness makes your heart and blood vessels strong and efficient, improves your endurance, and offers other benefits. Strength fitness makes you strong by strengthening the skeletal muscles as you work against resistance. Strength also offers the benefit of protecting you. Potential predators avoid the strong. I like that. And that happens without you realizing it or noticing it. But the bad guys notice and move on. I believe that any money spent on gym memberships or on running shoes is money well spent because the results are so beneficial.

Flexibility

A third form of fitness, one we all want to have especially as we become older, is what I would term flexibility. Flexibility is the ability to move in a wide range of motion in comfort and without becoming injured. The need for this is evident because with our modern lifestyle, we often don't move in a wide range of motion. It isn't built in. Many people sit at a desk or at a computer or telephone and don't move much in their jobs. When that happens, our connective tissues can shrink in length, particularly our tendons. What can happen as a result of that? Our range of motion can be reduced. In addition, we can become injured more easily. So if there is ever an emergency or you slip on a banana peel, you may make a wild or fast motion and injure yourself.

Therefore, it's wise to do flexibility exercises. These might be exercises such as stretching, yoga or other movement exercises. Stretching should be done gently and over a period of time. There should be no bouncing. Usually if you feel pain, it means you have gone too far, and you should back off a little bit. There are many stretching exercises. You can find them in books or online, in classes at your local gym and you probably learned some in your gym classes as a student.

Another form of flexibility exercise is yoga. Yoga is a great system of exercise, and it does wonderful things in terms of developing or improving flexibility. In fact, if you pick up a yoga book, you may see some postures that you will be amazed that people can get into. But with practice, the connective tissues grow in length, the flexibility improves a great deal, and a person can get into those postures and do it easily and comfortably. Then if you ever slip on a banana peel, you might get hurt when you hit the ground, but you are unlikely to injure yourself because of the quick motion.

Skill

A fourth form of fitness is skill. Skill at performing a task improves as a result of practice and lots of practice. Sports like karate, figure-skating, shooting a basketball, gymnastics and others often lead to the development of high levels of skill. Practice and repetition is the key to developing and improving skill of any kind. Practice improves both precision and quickness while reducing errors. With much practice people develop high levels of ability. It's amazing what level of skill some people are able to develop.

One of my favorite sayings along those lines goes like this:

"Before you can be great, you have to be good.

Before you can be good, you have to be bad [as in

unskilled].

And before you can be bad, you have to try."

And isn't that the way people learn most things? That through practice and lots of practice, we develop high levels of skill if that is our wish. Most sports are pretty optional. Most people do not do gymnastics or figure skating or playing the piano at an accomplished level such as a concert pianist. The skills we each develop are by individual choice and often sports or activities we love doing because then we can do lots of practicing while having fun at the same time. At times like that, practicing is not a chore but is actually recreation.

Some of my favorite stories illustrate this learning sequence. Michael Jordan, one of the greatest players ever to play basketball, was cut from his high school basketball team as a sophomore. He could have said, "I stink" and quit. He forced himself to serve as team manager that year. But he kept working at it. He grew taller and improved his skills. And he went from being a beginner to good and later great. And perhaps he became the greatest player of all time as his record shows. A part of his story that few people know is that as a college player at North Carolina, he did some extra work at each practice. He would do 120 dunks prior to practice as part of his warm-up routine. Is there any doubt that with that kind of practice, he would become an outstanding leaper and dunker of basketballs?

Albert Einstein was once considered a mediocre math student. He didn't like math, he thought. Or maybe just he just didn't like his math class. But years later, as he understood the usefulness of mathematics, he became quite excellent at math to the point where his name is synonymous with genius. It wasn't always that way.

So if you lack skill in a certain area. Realize it isn't you. You are just on a temporary lower level on that continuum and that with practice and lots of practice, you can develop as high a level of skill as you wish.

One skill that should be universal would be to have some self-defense skills in the event that you are encounter a bad guy. It is good to have these available if you ever find yourself in an emergency situation and need to escape. Being strong and fit helps as well. The reality is there are some evil people in the world who may seek to victimize others. So I would recommend that you develop some skills that you practice just in case you find yourself in a position where you would want to escape from an attacker or a dangerous situation. It's good to be prepared as the boy scouts say. The universe is a funny and an amazing place. Once you have self defense skill, you will probably never need to use it. It's almost as if people know, and they will not bother you. It's amazing.

Since I studied karate, which was in like 1976, nobody has ever bothered me. So I've never ever had to use these skills except as a form of exercise. That is pretty amazing since this is over forty years later, and I live in the New York City metropolitan area. So it had a very wonderful effect in my own personal experience. It is also true that for most of that time, I trained and kept myself fit and strong and muscular as well. And as I wrote earlier, bad guys tend to avoid those who look strong and able to defend themselves.

I believe it is desirable to be fit and strong, be aware of your surroundings, and develop some basic self-defense skills. And hopefully you, like me, will never need to use them.

To summarize, I'd say that probably the best form of fitness is aerobic fitness because it enables you to benefit in a number of ways. You will look good, feel good, have great endurance, enjoy your chosen sports, be strong, control your weight, develop skill, enjoy the emotional benefits of the above, and make friends all at the same time. Talk about multitasking. And you can develop excellent fitness using just a few minutes a day to train.

Main point: Physical fitness is well worth the effort and time you devote to it. And you can be fit at any age.

CHAPTER 12: PATHS TO WEALTH OR POVERTY

Why are some people wealthy and others poor? That is a very important question and some of the reasons are obvious. I'll list a few and then say a few things about some of them.

Behaviors that lead toward wealth:

1. Living on less than you earn.
2. Saving and investing
3. Maintaining optimum health
4. Work and bring home income
5. Reading, learning and education
6. Religion, the Bible, faith and principled morality
7. Giving
8. Helping and serving others
9. Obeying the rules, laws and Commandments and thus staying out of trouble.
10. Honesty and keeping your word.

Behaviors that lead toward poverty:

1. Credit cards and excessive spending

2. DEBT

3. Alcohol and drugs

4. Smoking

5. Crime and violence

6. Gambling

7. Divorce, single or unwed pregnancy

8. Serious illness, accidents and disability

9. Old age if financially unprepared.

10.   Lack of a complete education.

11.   Spending all you earn.

12.   Lying, cheating and breaking your word.

Main point:

The poor may always be with us, but you don't have to be one of them. Embrace the habits that lead to wealth while also avoiding those choices and behaviors that lead toward poverty.

The above lists and behaviors are fairly obvious yet people stumble into some of the negative ones without understanding the implications. Debt and credit cards are heavily marketed to us constantly. So it is important to understand how they can harm us, our finances and our loved ones. Debt may create a momentary high when we buy that new item, but it is delaying gratification, saving up and paying cash, saving and investing that can produce the best results and build wealth for our futures. And that can last a lifetime and even generations.

I'm wishing you all the best.

Charles D Calhoun

9 781734 219708